Toys

Contents

 Look and put the sticker.

doll

robot

ball

blocks

 Put sticker on the word.

Do you have a [ball] ?

Yes, I do.

 Ask and say.

 Color and say.

 robot

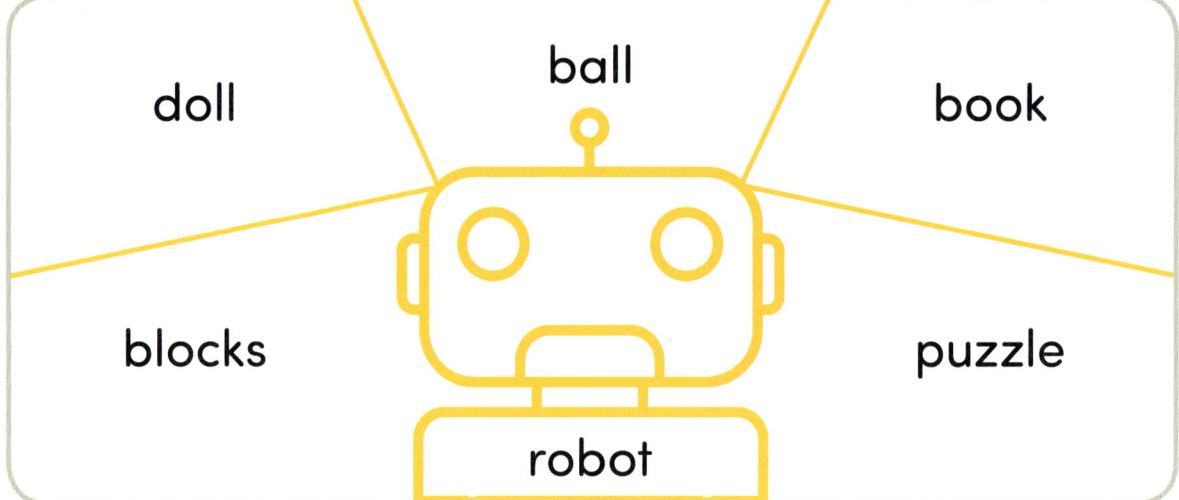

doll

ball

book

blocks

puzzle

robot

 blocks

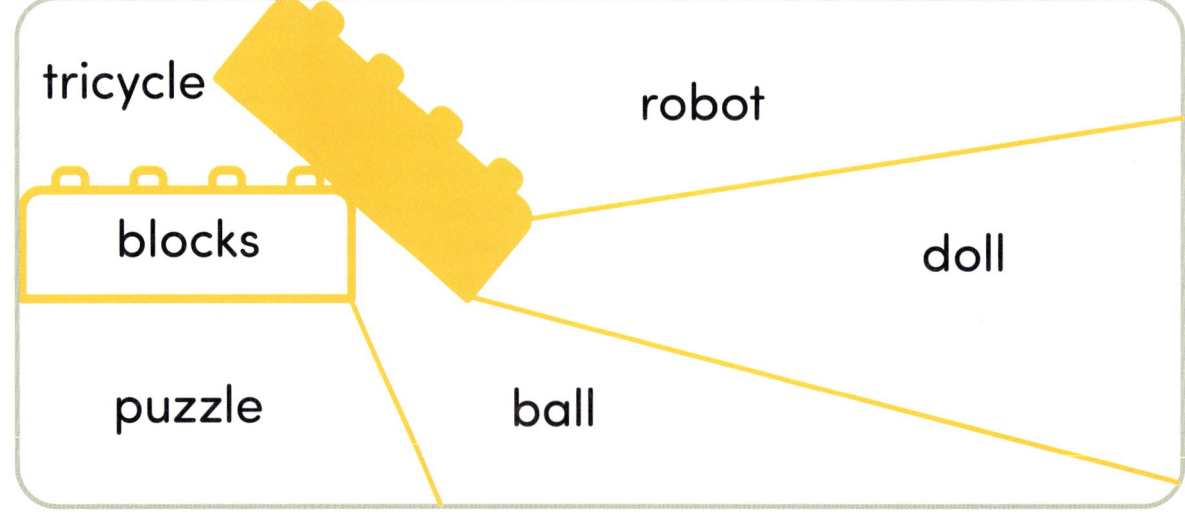

tricycle

robot

blocks

doll

puzzle

ball

Let's Learn

 Look and put the sticker.

puzzle

book

tricycle

car

 **Put sticker on the word.**

Do you have a puzzle ?

No, I don't.

 Ask and say.

 p. 2

 p. 3 **ball**

 p. 5

 p. 6 **puzzle**

 Sticker

 Good work!

 Wonderful work!

 Great effort!

 For working hard!

 Good work!

 Excellent!

 Well done!

 Well done!

 Special award!

Find and circle.

doll

book

Organize the toys on the shelf.

book	ball
blocks	puzzle

car

robot

tricycle

doll